My Path to Math

123456789

SUBTRACTION

Ann Becker

Crabtree Publishing Company

www.crabtreebooks.com

Author: Ann Becker
Coordinating editor: Chester Fisher
Series editor: Penny Dowdy
Editor: Reagan Miller
Proofreader: Ellen Rodger
Editorial director: Kathy Middleton
Production coordinator: Margaret Amy Salter
Prepress technician: Margaret Amy Salter
Cover design: Samara Parent
Logo design: Samantha Crabtree
Project manager: Kumar Kunal (Q2AMEDIA)
Art direction: Dibakar Acharjee (Q2AMEDIA)
Design: Supriya Manna (Q2AMEDIA)
Photo research: Poulomi Basu (Q2AMEDIA)

Photographs:
123RF: Joao Estevao Freitas: p. 17, 20; Joshua Haviv: p. 23 (left);
    Cathy Keifer: p. 17
Dreamstime: Chartchai Meesangnin: p. 17
Istockphoto: Brian Evans: p. 20; Marek Mierzejewski: p. 20;
    Jarek Szymanski: p. 12; William Walsh: p. 15
Photolibrary: Shamel Ann: p. 4, 8, 23 (right)
Q2AMedia Art Bank: p. 5, 7, 9, 10, 11, 14, 21, 22, folio image
Shutterstock: p. 15, 17, 19, 21; ArchMan: p. 15; Timothy Boomer:
    front cover (bottom right); Aron Brand: p. 15, 19; Chris Brink: p. 7;
    Norma Cornes: p. 11; Neale Cousland: p. 15, 19; DLW-Designs:
    p. 15; Elena Elisseeva: p. 13; Melissa King: p. 19; Kruchankova
    Maya: p. 19 (top); V. J. Matthew: p. 5, 9; Thomas M Perkins:
    front cover (center); Matka Wariatka: p. 1

Library and Archives Canada Cataloguing in Publication

Becker, Ann, 1965-
    Subtraction / Ann Becker.

(My path to math)
Includes index.
ISBN 978-0-7787-4350-7 (bound).--ISBN 978-0-7787-4368-2 (pbk.)

    1. Subtraction--Juvenile literature. I. Title. II. Series:
My path to math

QA115.B426 2009   j513.2'12   C2009-903579-0

Library of Congress Cataloging-in-Publication Data

Becker, Ann, 1965-
    Subtraction / Ann Becker.
        p. cm. -- (My path to math)
    Includes index.
    ISBN 978-0-7787-4350-7 (reinforced lib. bdg. : alk. paper)
    -- ISBN 978-0-7787-4368-2 (pbk. : alk. paper)
    1. Subtraction--Juvenile literature. I. Title. II. Series.

    QA115.B434 2010
    513.2'12--dc22

                                                2009022857

Crabtree Publishing Company
www.crabtreebooks.com   1-800-387-7650

Published in Canada
Crabtree Publishing
616 Welland Ave.
St. Catharines, ON
L2M 5V6

Published in the United States
Crabtree Publishing
PMB16A
350 Fifth Ave., Suite 3308
New York, NY 10118

Published in the United Kingdom
Crabtree Publishing
Lorna House, Suite 3.03, Lorna Road
Hove, East Sussex, UK
BN3 3EL

Published in Australia
Crabtree Publishing
386 Mt. Alexander Rd.
Ascot Vale (Melbourne)
VIC 3032

Contents

How Many More?

June loves butterflies. She visits them at the park. Caterpillars eat the plants. They build cocoons. Then beautiful butterflies come out!

This week 3 butterflies hatched from their cocoons. Last week, 5 butterflies hatched. June wants to know how many more butterflies hatched last week? The words "how many more" tell June to **subtract**.

▲ 5 hatched last week

▲ 3 hatched this week

June watches the butterflies hatch.

Subtraction Words

Words like, "How many more?" tell June to subtract. Other subtraction words are:

Subtraction Words	Example
difference	What is the **difference** between 5 and 3?
take away	What is 5 **take away** 3?
how much less	**How much less** is 3 than 5?
minus	Subtract 5 **minus** 3.
how many are left	**How many are left** when you subtract 3 from 5?

Fact Box

Can you make a question using subtraction words?

6

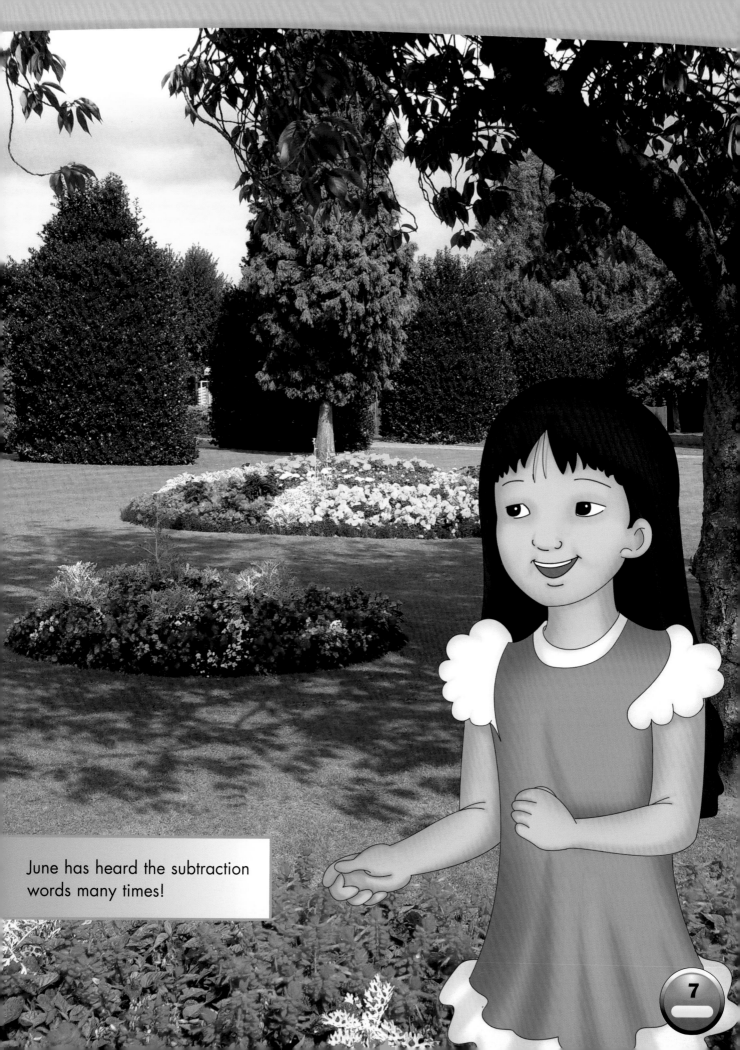

June has heard the subtraction words many times!

Comparing

Tim works with the butterflies. He is June's friend.

Tim talks about **comparing**. When you compare, you look at two groups. You chose which group has more. Then you tell how many more this group has.

Look at the two groups of cocoons.
Five cocoons is more than three cocoons.
The group of 5 cocoons has 2 more
cocoons than the group of 3.

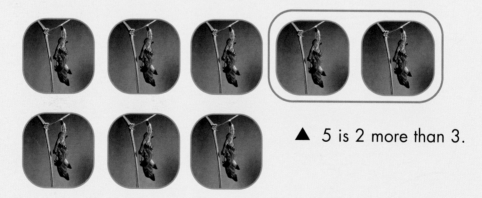

▲ 5 is 2 more than 3.

Fact Box

The answer to a subtraction problem
is called the **difference**.

Tim tells June
how to compare.

Take Away

June asks Tim to teach her more about subtraction. Tim says that subtraction is also taking things away.

Tim asks, "Do you see 7 butterflies by the flowers? What if 3 flew away?"

June tries taking away. She starts with 7. Then she takes 3 away. She counts back: 6, 5, 4. So 7 minus 3 is 4!

▲ The number line shows how June subtracts as Tim counts back.

Fact Box

Five butterflies land on a tree. One flew away. Is this comparing or take away?

June subtracts when butterflies fly away.

Write Subtraction

Tim shows June how to write subtraction problems. Tim writes subtraction with a **symbol**. It is called a **minus sign**. It looks like this: −

Tim tells June that she can use the minus sign to write her own subtraction problems.

June uses **unit blocks** to help her solve subtraction problems. Numbers take the place of the unit blocks. Tim subtracts 7 from 8 on paper.
8 − 7

Count back with Tim to find the answer:
7, 6, 5, 4, 3, 2, 1.

8 − 7 = 1
So 8 minus 7 equals 1!

June writes the
subtraction problem!

8 − 7 = 1

Up and Down

You can write the subtraction problem a different way. You use numbers. But you can write the problem up and down.

Numbers can stand for a **number line**, too. June writes 6 minus 2. She starts with 6.

6
-   June writes the minus sign.

6
-2   Now she writes the 2.
⎯   She draws a line underneath it.

6
-2
⎯   Count back with June to
4   find the answer: 5, 4.

How many butterflies are left if 4 fly away?

Fact Box

Write the subtraction problem "eight minus four" two different ways.

What is Missing?

Tim puts caterpillars in cages.
They will build cocoons soon.

He has 12 cages ready. He puts a caterpillar in 7 cages. How many more caterpillars does he need to find to fill the empty cages?

Subtraction can help solve this problem. You know that $7 + \_ = 12$. We can do subtraction using the two numbers we do know to find the missing number.

$12 - 7 = \_\_$

Compare or count back to find the difference. 11, 10, 9, 8, 7, 6, 5. Tim needs 5 more caterpillars to fill the empty cages.

$12 - 7 = 5$

Tim puts caterpillars in cages to keep them safe while they hatch.

Subtraction Rules

June is excited to learn more about subtraction. Tim teaches June two important subtraction rules.

Rule 1: A number minus the same number equals 0.

Tim has 7 cocoons. All 7 cocoons hatch. How many are left? Zero!
$7 - 7 = 0$

Rule 2: A number minus zero stays the same. The number does not change.

June sees 5 butterflies resting in a tree. None of the butterflies fly away. How many butterflies are in the tree?
$5 - 0 = 5$
There are still five butterflies in the tree.

Seven cocoons were on the branch. All seven hatched. How many cocoons are left?

Four butterflies visit the flowers. Zero butterflies fly away. How many are left?

Subtract with Me!

June likes subtracting. Tim gives her two problems to try. Grab a pencil and join June in solving these subtraction problems!

Tim holds 16 caterpillars. He hands 8 to June.

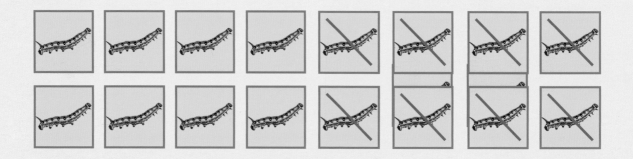

How many caterpillars does Tim have now? June sees 10 black butterflies. Then she sees 1 blue butterfly. How many more black butterflies does she see?

June can now solve subtraction problems in different ways.

Glossary

compare To tell which number is more or less

difference The answer to a subtraction problem

minus sign −

number line

1   2   3   4   5   6

subtract To take away from a number or compare two numbers

symbol Something that stands for
something else

unit blocks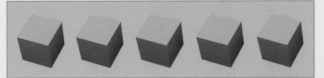

Index

AUG 2 4 2016

Printed in the U.S.A. — BG